ROMAN
TIMES

A VILLA

well

kitchen

courtyard

a living room

barn

ception room

JEWELLERY

beads

bracelets

brooch

charms

chains

rings

pins

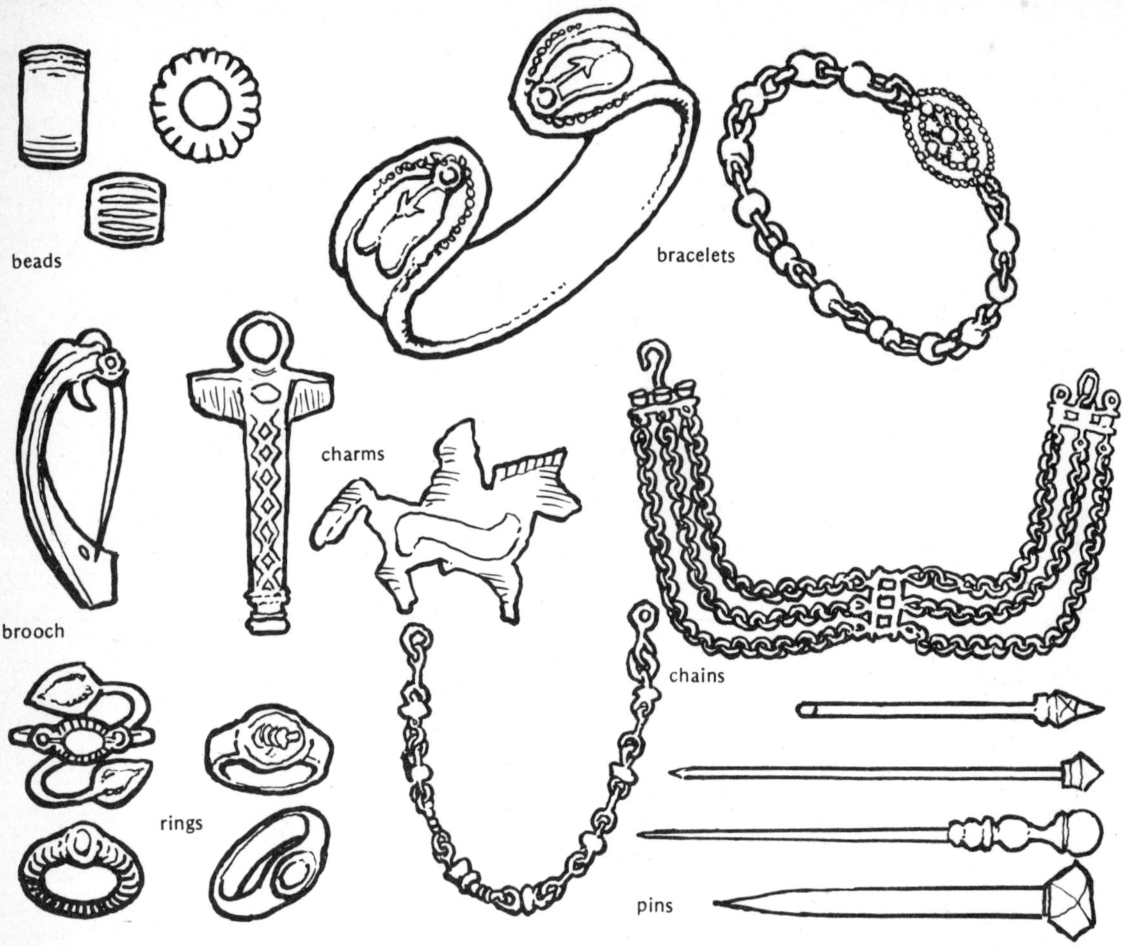

ACCESSORIES

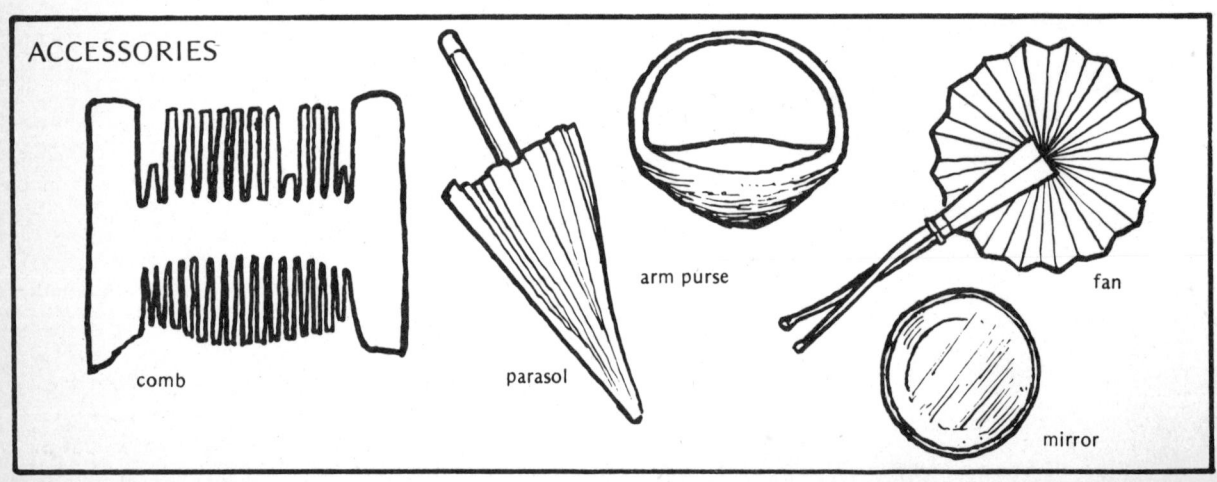

comb

parasol

arm purse

fan

mirror

CLOTHES

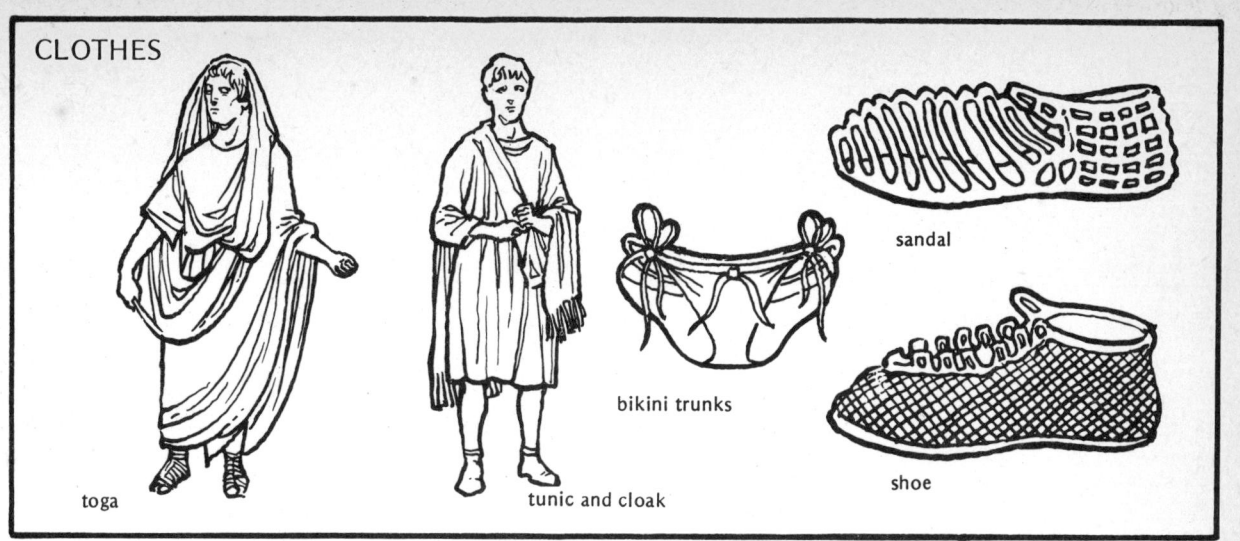

toga

tunic and cloak

bikini trunks

sandal

shoe

DWELLINGS

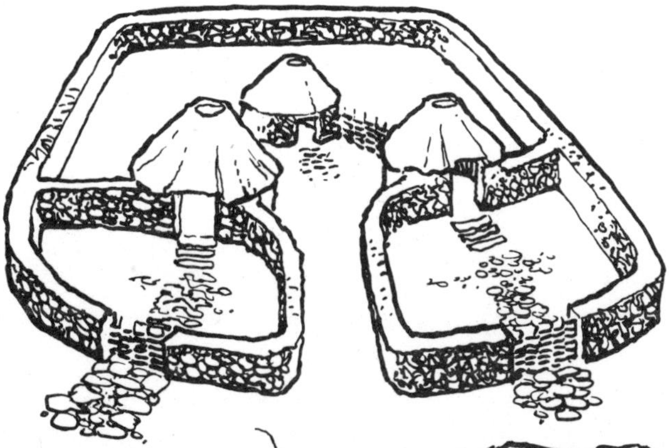

farmstead

broch

farm

POTTERY AND PEWTER

cooking p

pottery jug

pottery beaker

bowl

gridiron

GLASSWARE

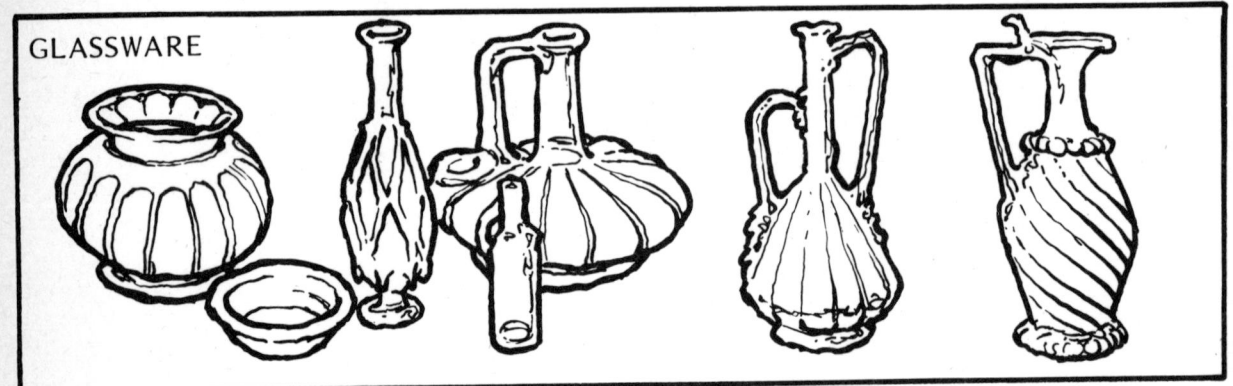

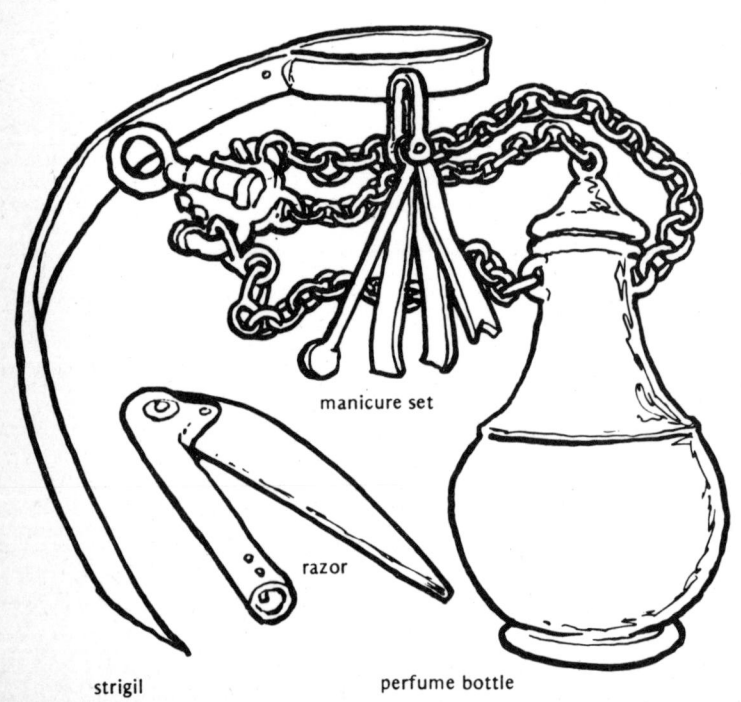

manicure set

razor

strigil

perfume bottle

COSMETICS

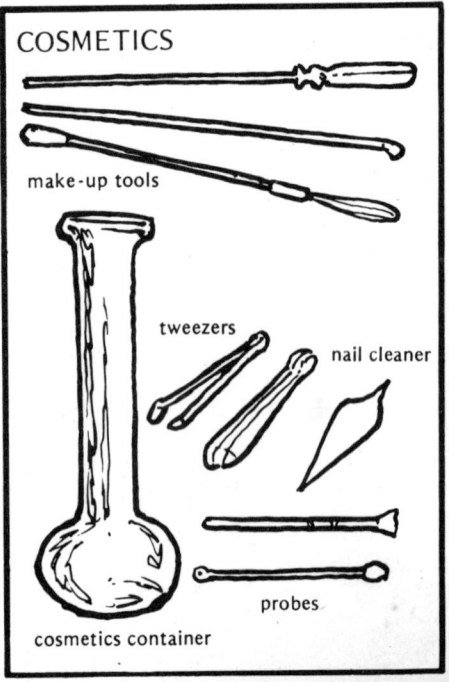

make-up tools

tweezers

nail cleaner

cosmetics container

probes

bowls   pewter box   bowls

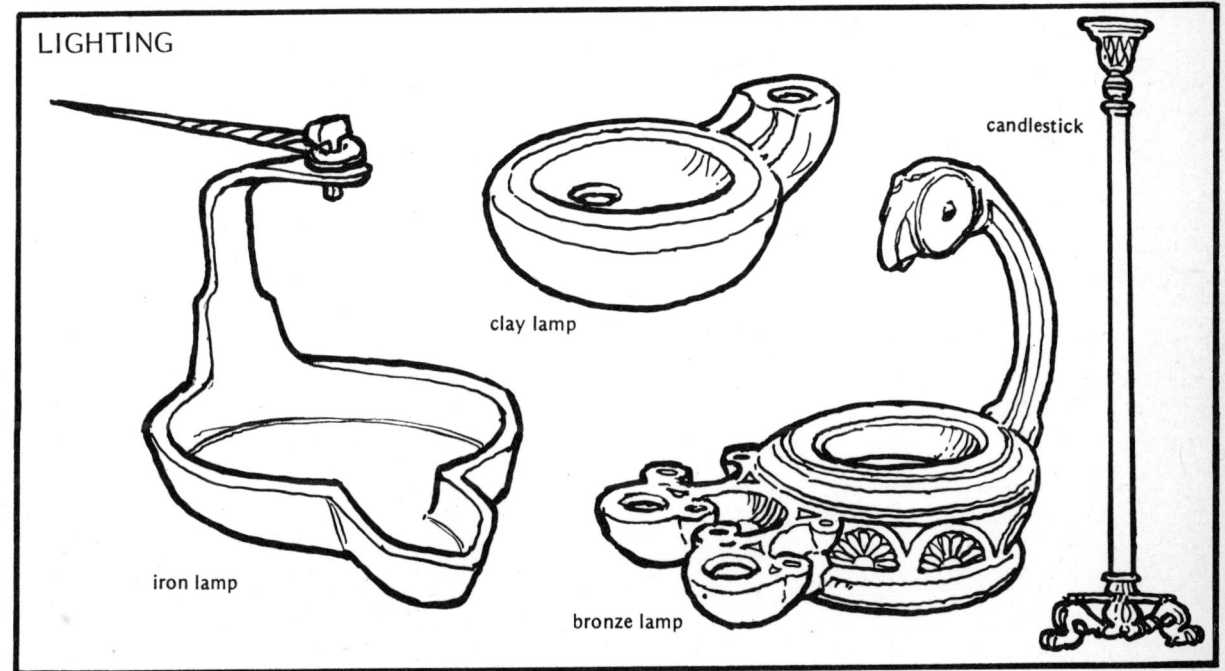

LIGHTING

candlestick

clay lamp

iron lamp

bronze lamp

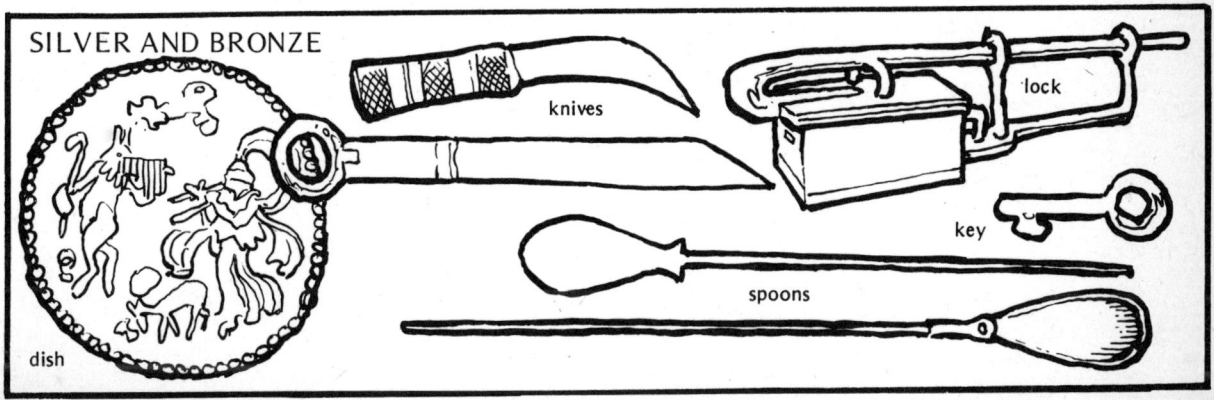

SILVER AND BRONZE

knives

lock

key

spoons

dish

ROMAN TIMES **Working Life**

POTTERY

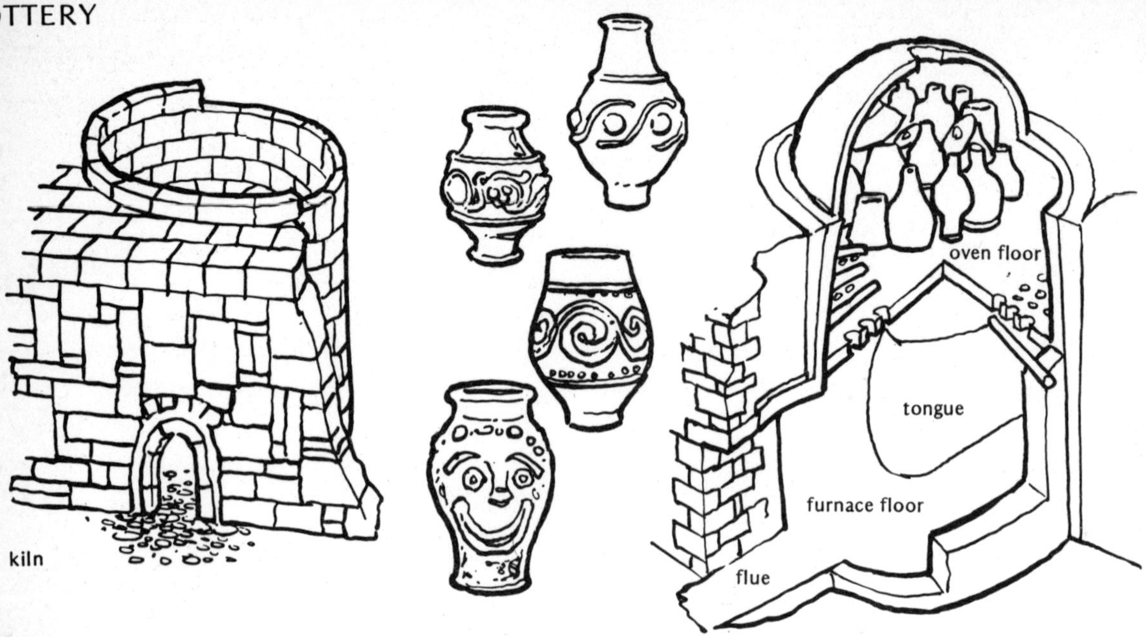
kiln
oven floor
tongue
furnace floor
flue

THE SMITHY

hammer
blacksmith
pincers

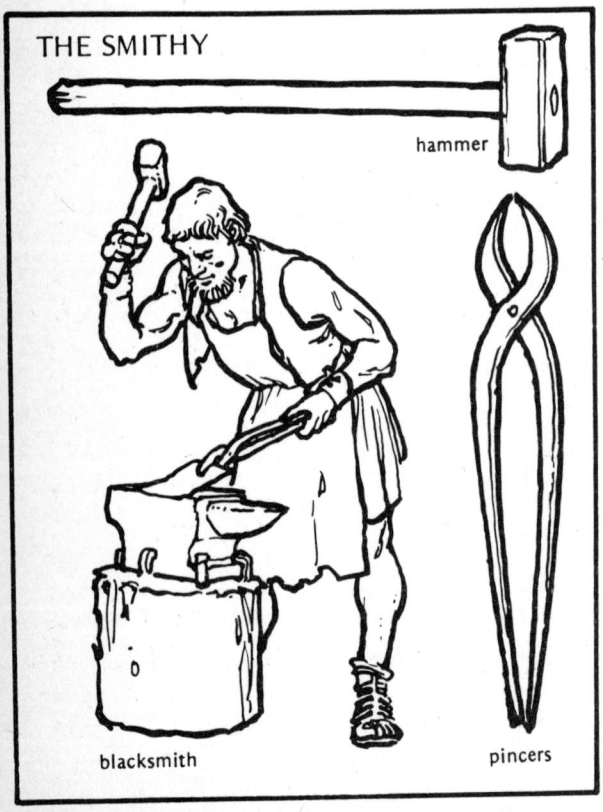

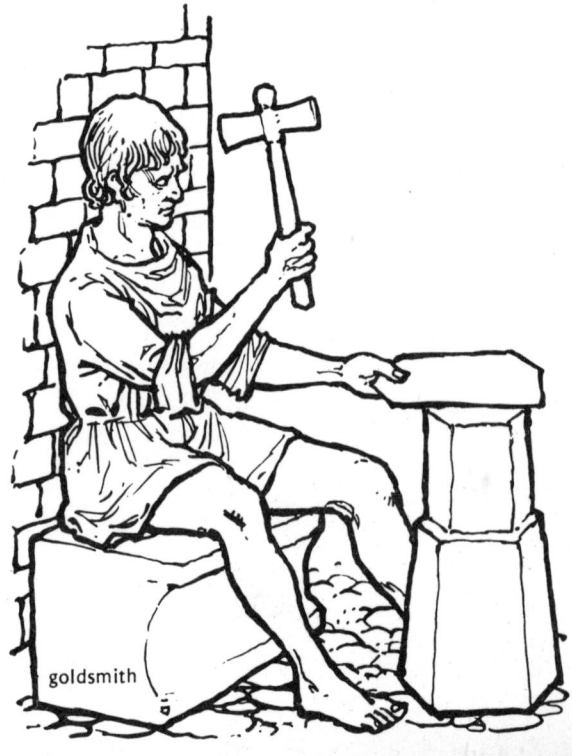

goldsmith

SHOPPING

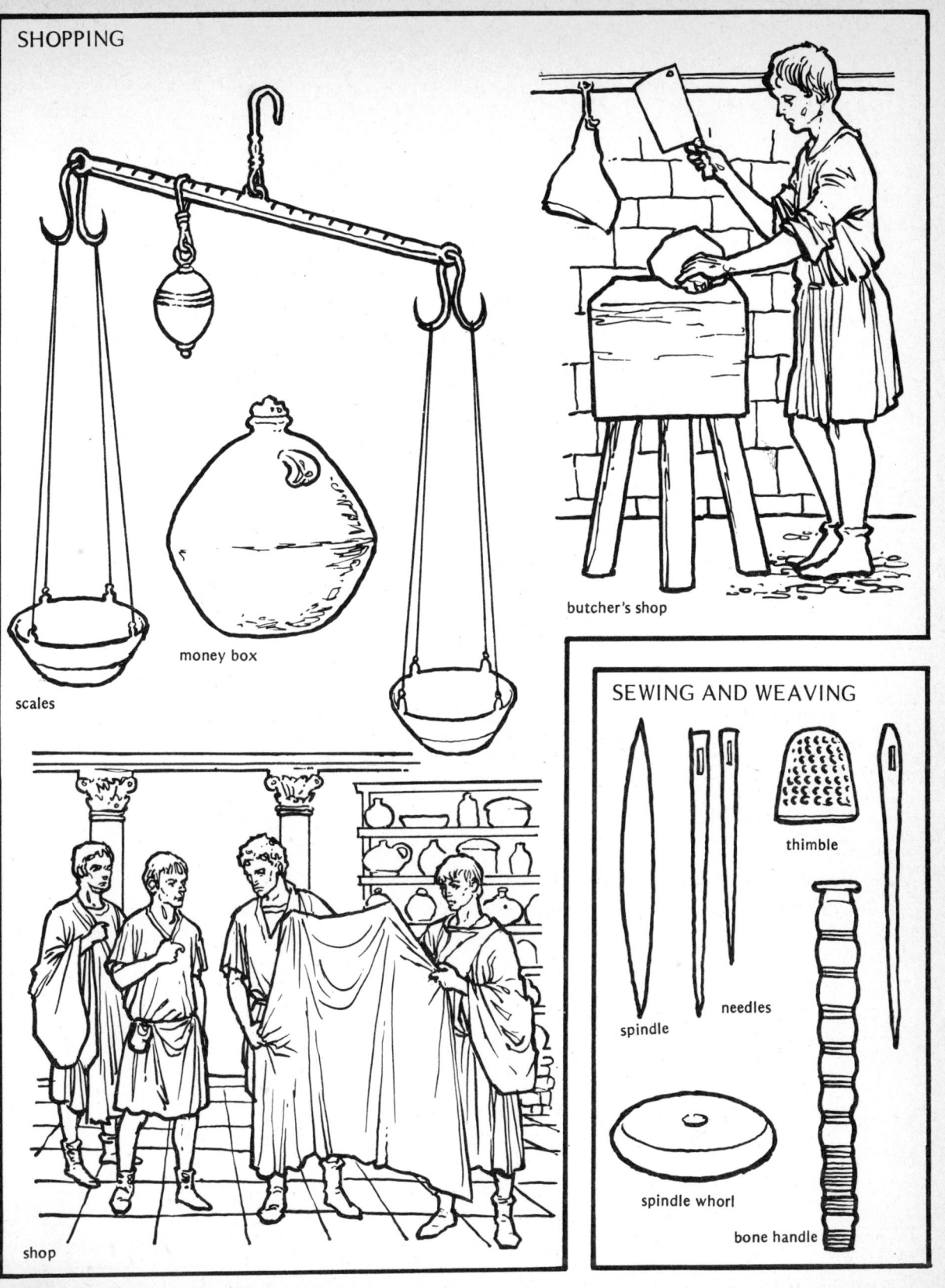

scales

money box

butcher's shop

shop

SEWING AND WEAVING

spindle

needles

thimble

spindle whorl

bone handle

AGRICULTURE

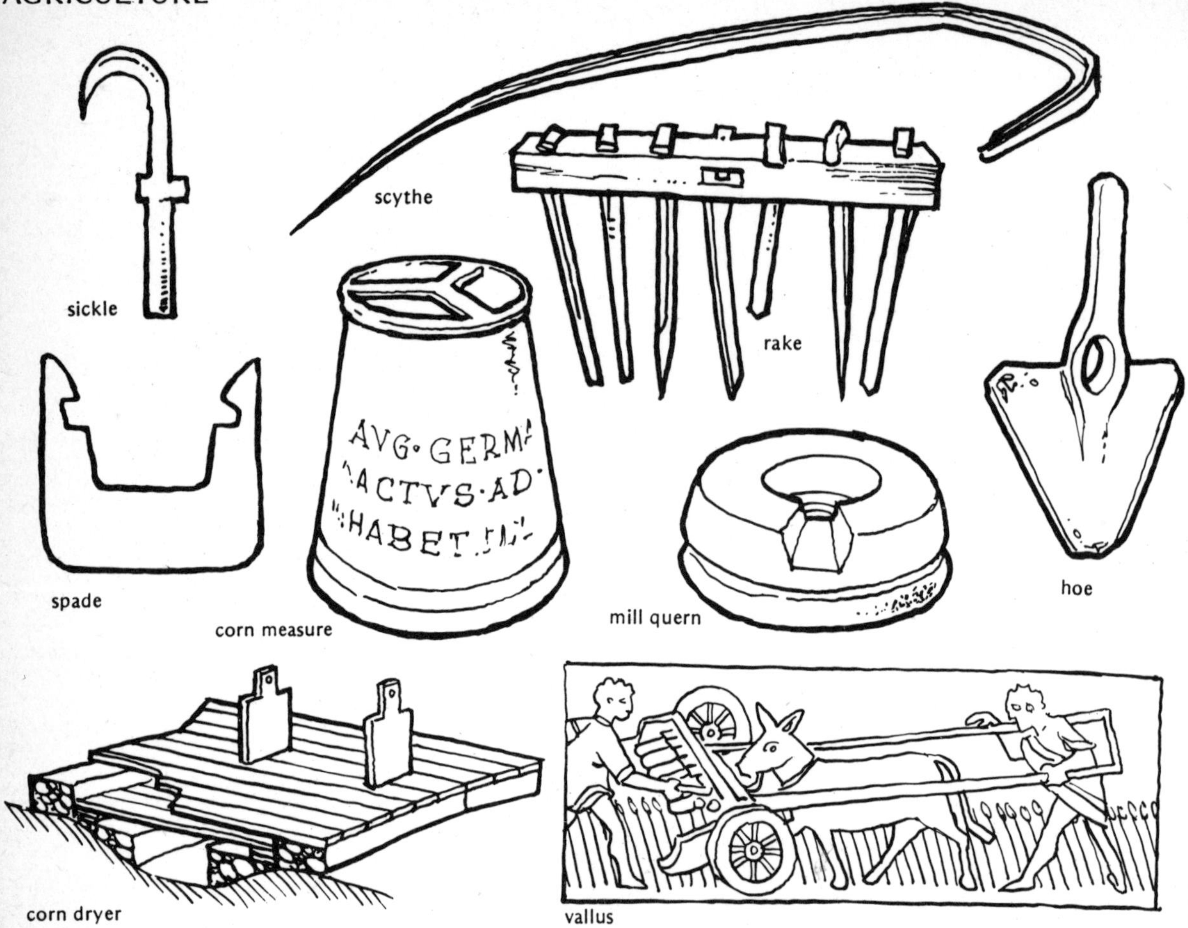

sickle

scythe

rake

spade

corn measure

AVG·GERMᴬ
ᴬACTVS·AD·
ᴴHABET·Iᴺ

mill quern

hoe

corn dryer

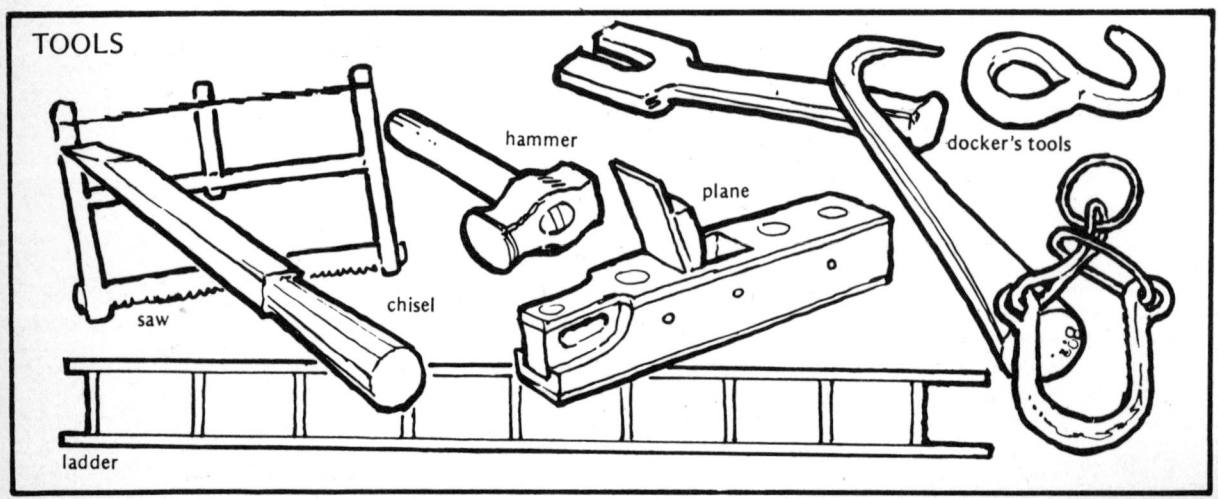

vallus

TOOLS

saw

hammer

chisel

plane

docker's tools

ladder

ROMAN LEADERS

Julius Caesar   Claudius   Hadrian   Septimus Severus

procurator's seal

metal stamp

medallions

Hadrian's coin

Claudius's coin

reverse of Hadrian's coin

coin of Antonius Pius

BRITONS

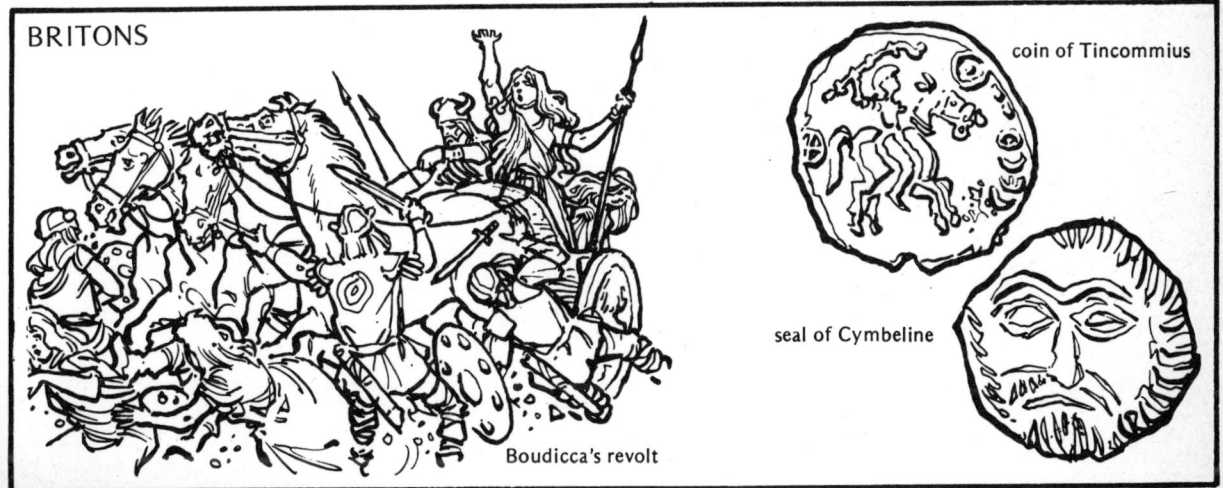

Boudicca's revolt

coin of Tincommius

seal of Cymbeline

BUILDING A ROMAN ROAD

clay base

hard gravel

cobbles and gravel   sand   quarry stones   quarry stones

yellow sand or chippings

VEHICLES

pack mule

Celtic chariot

Roman chariot

cart

milestone

HORSEWARE

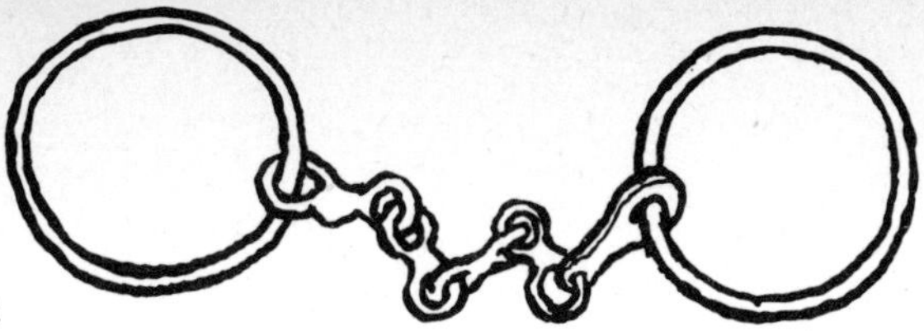

bit

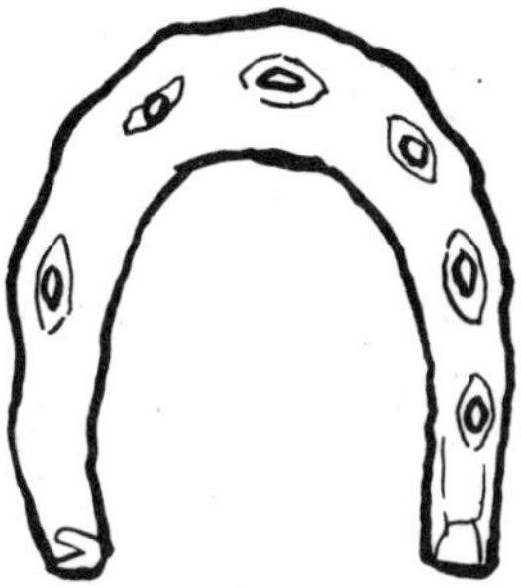

horseshoe

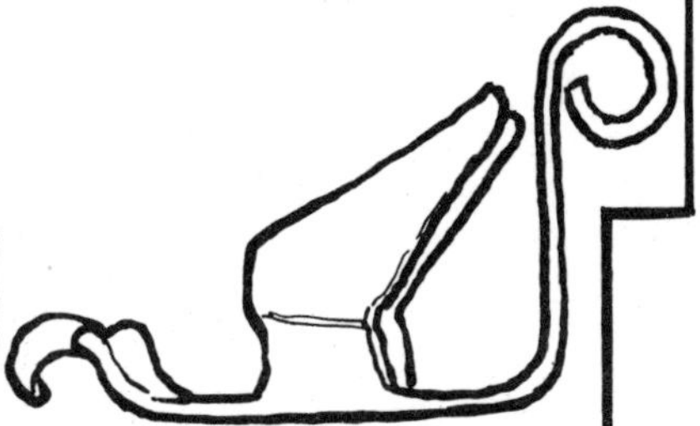

hipposandal

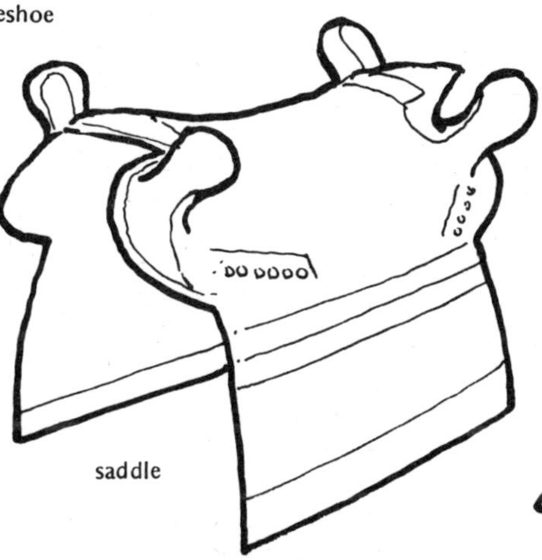

saddle

spur

lighthouse

WATER TRANSPORT

merchant ship

barge

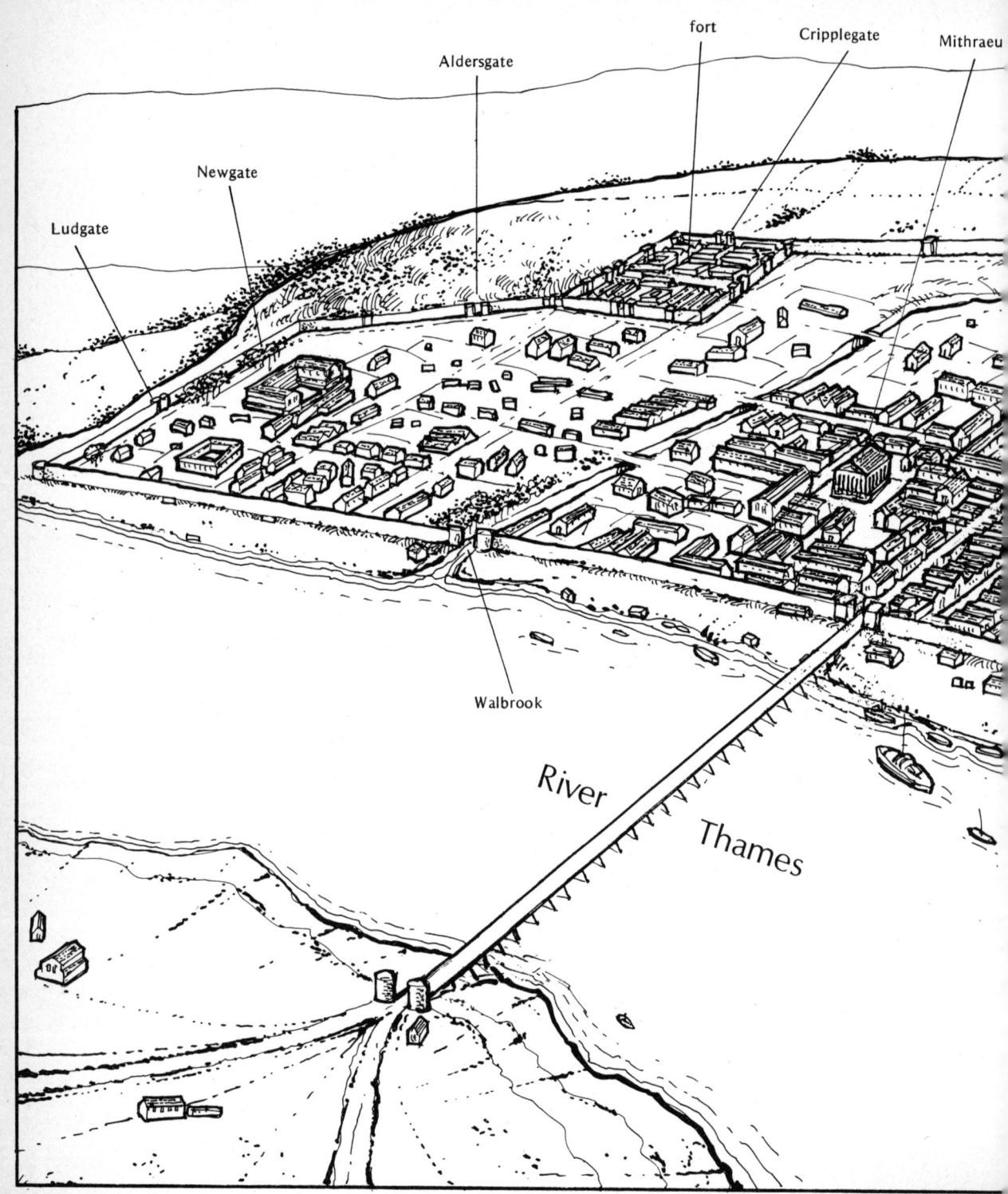

Ludgate

Newgate

Aldersgate

fort

Cripplegate

Mithraeu

Walbrook

River

Thames

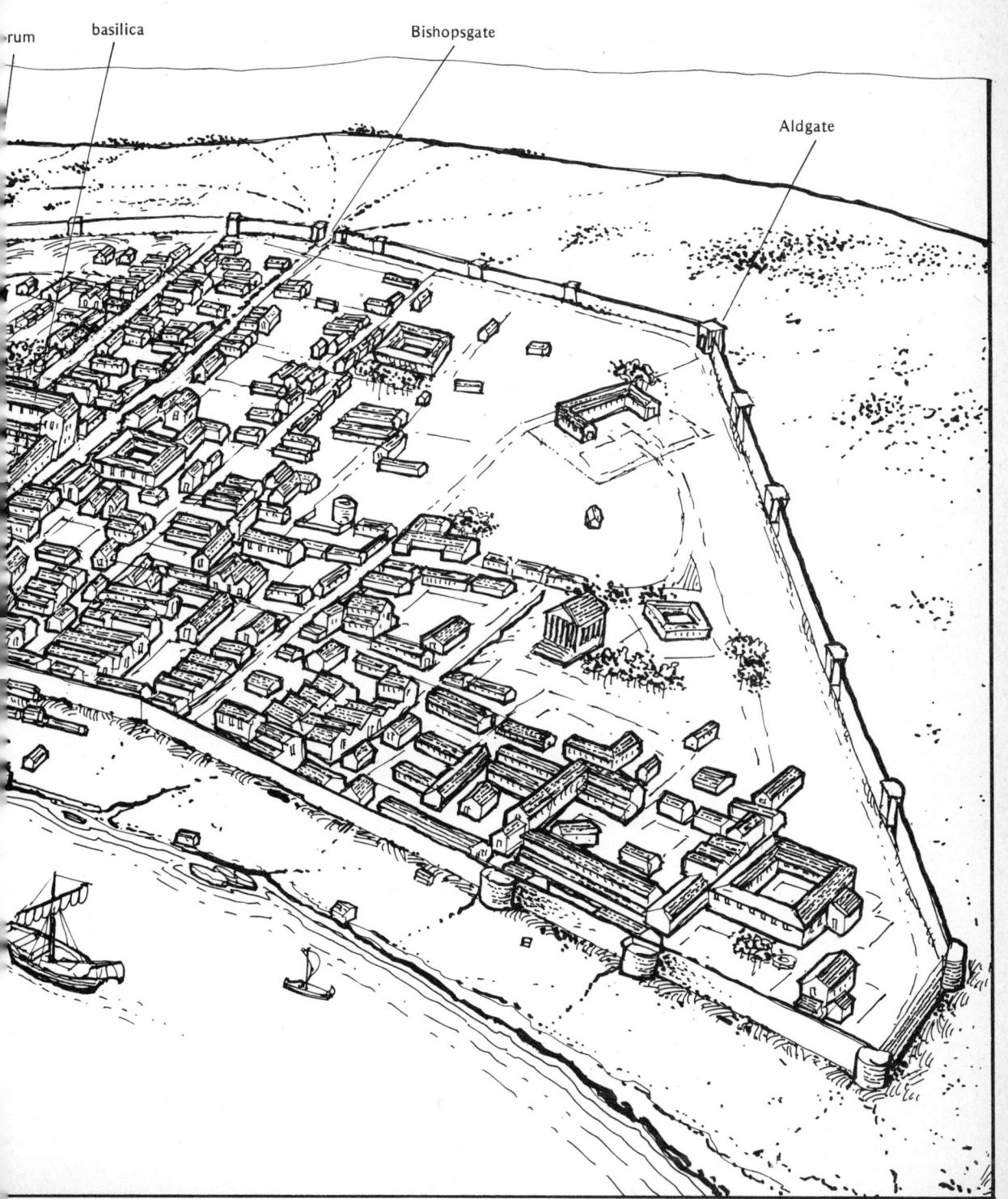

rum basilica Bishopsgate Aldgate

ROMAN GODS

Minerva

Venus

river god

Mithras

Mercury

Cybele

Serapis

Bacchus

Horus

Taranus

CELTIC CULT HEADS

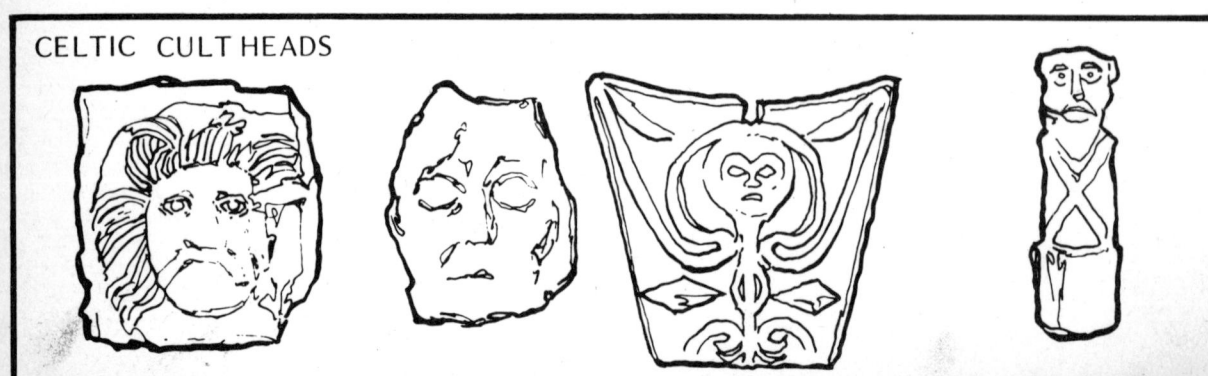

TEMPLES

Romano-Celtic

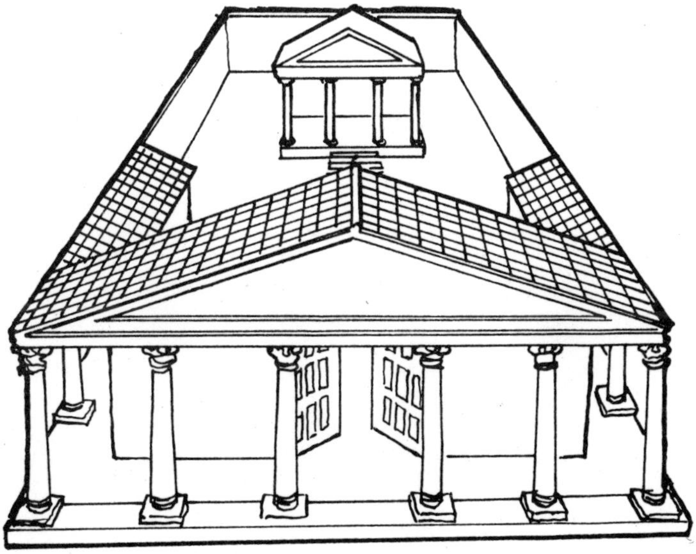

Classical

Imperial

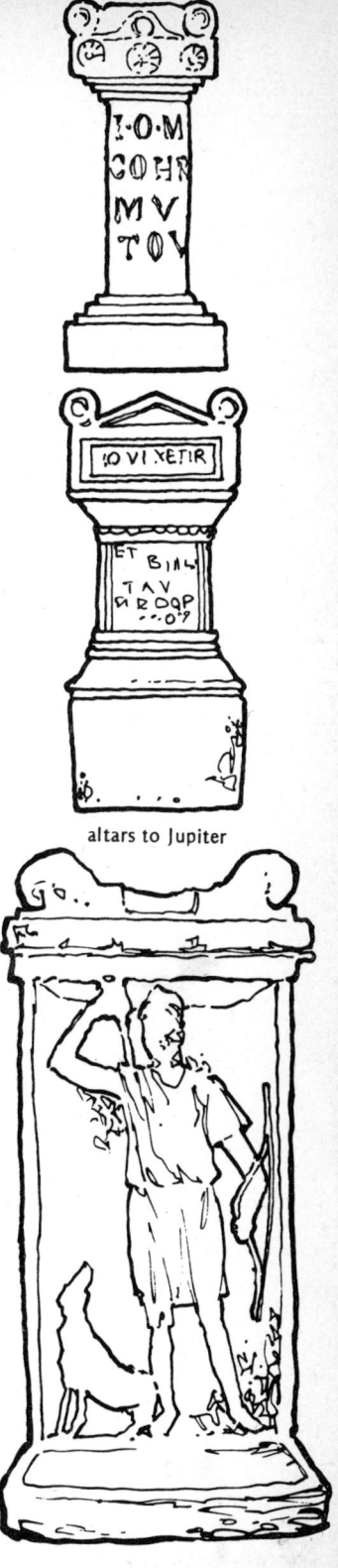

altars to Jupiter

altar to Diana

TOMBS AND MONUMENTS

funerary sphinx

funeral urns

legionary's tombstone

coffins

priest

PUBLIC WORKS

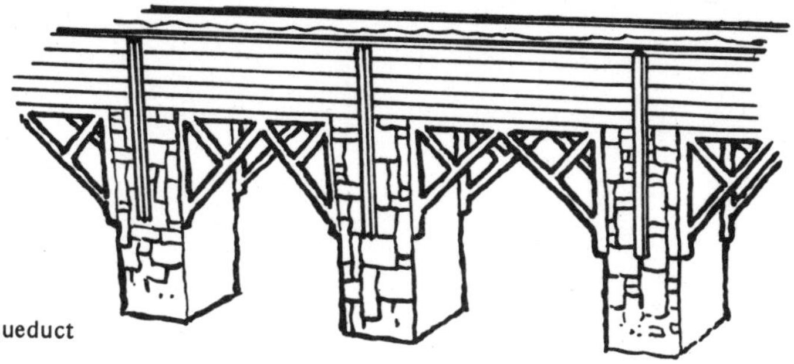

aqueduct

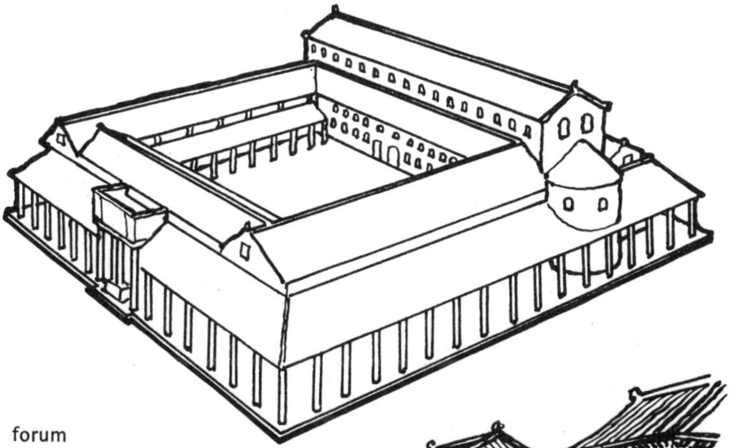

forum

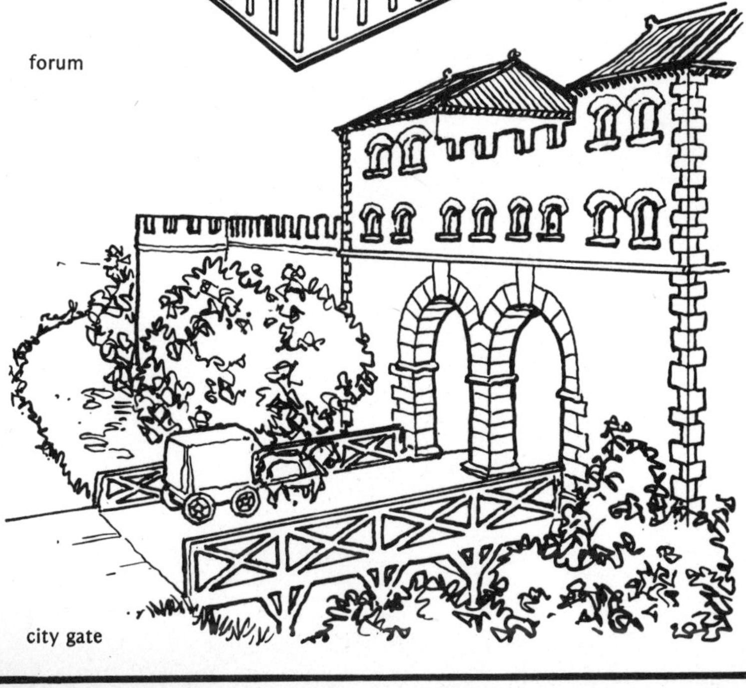

city gate

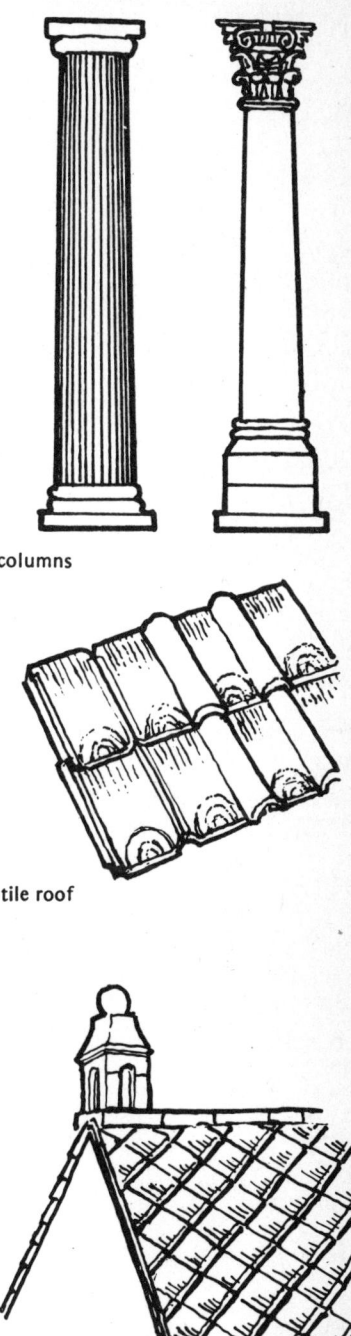

columns

tile roof

slate roof

ROMAN TIMES   **Military Life**

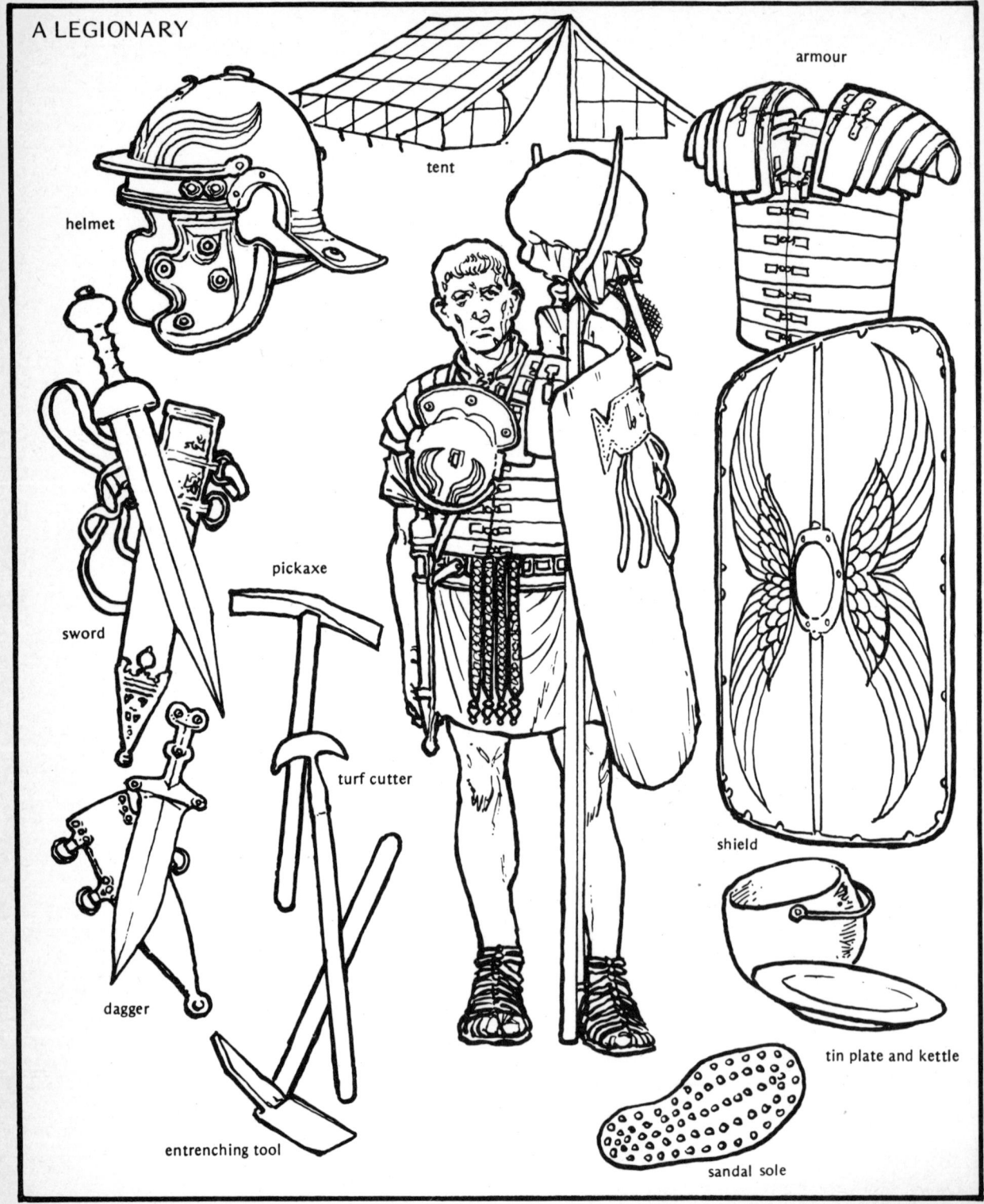

A LEGIONARY

tent

armour

helmet

sword

pickaxe

turf cutter

dagger

shield

entrenching tool

tin plate and kettle

sandal sole

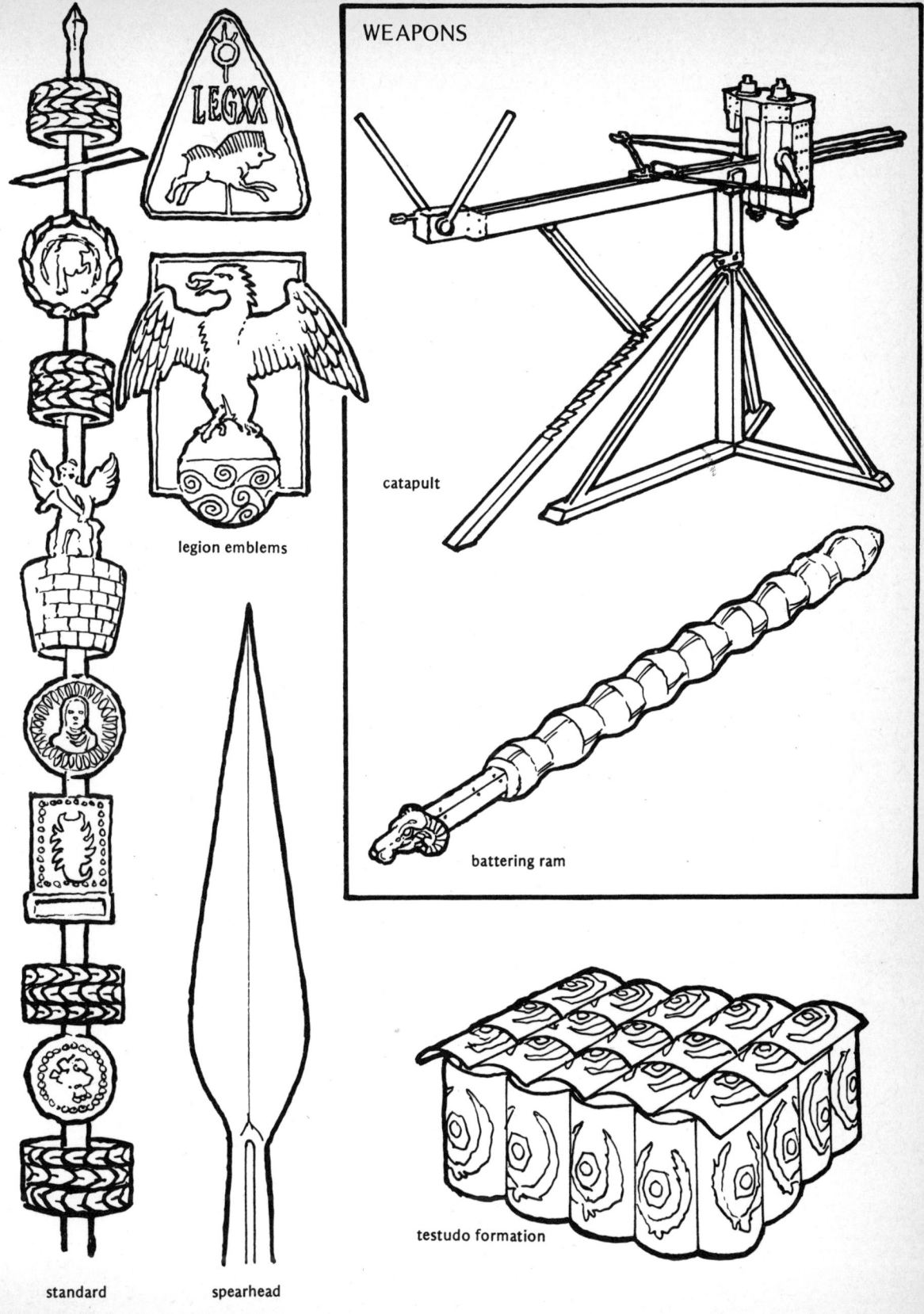

WEAPONS

LEGXX

legion emblems

catapult

battering ram

standard

spearhead

testudo formation

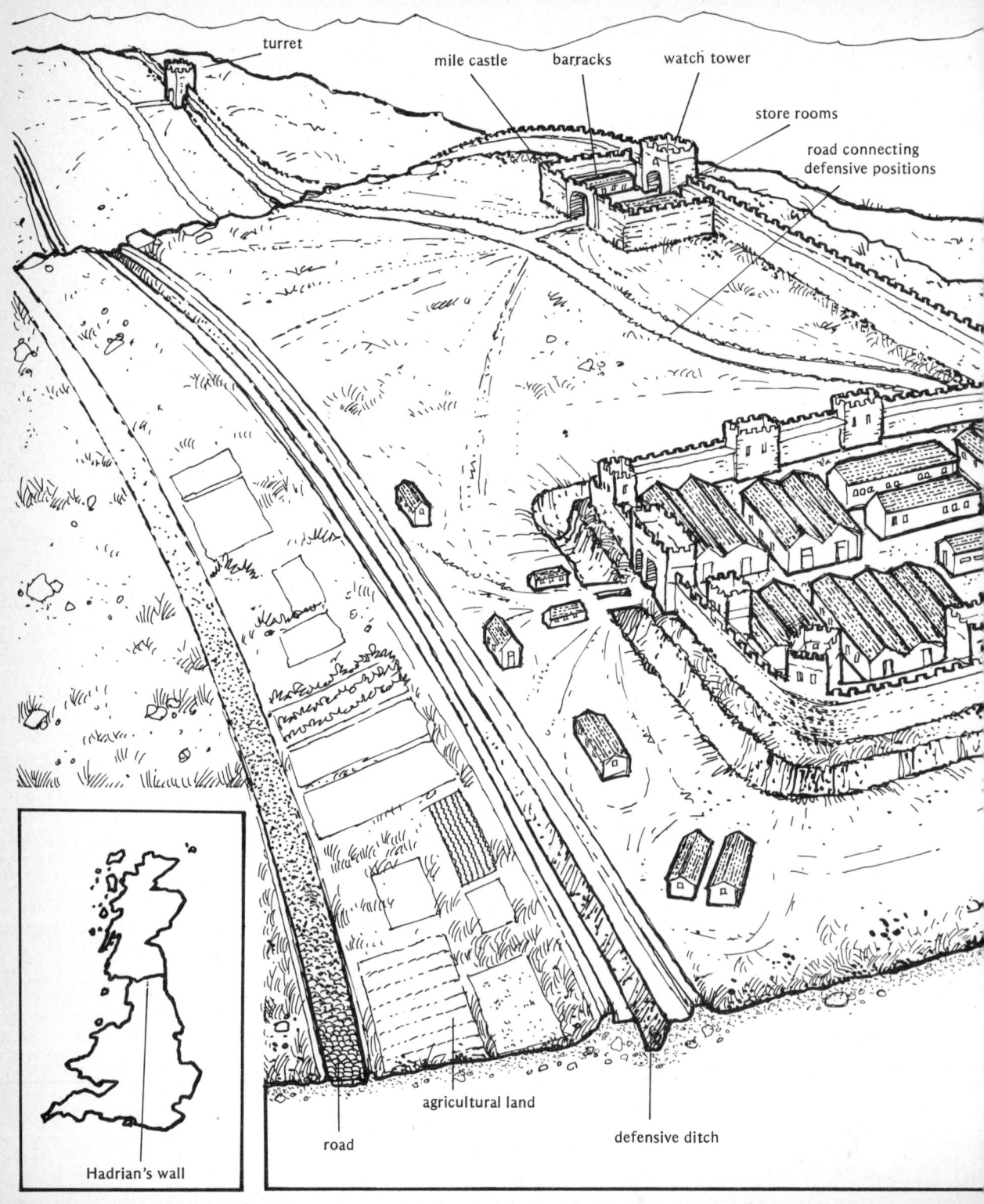

ROMAN TIMES   Hadrian's Wall

turret

mile castle

barracks

watch tower

store rooms

road connecting
defensive positions

agricultural land

road

defensive ditch

Hadrian's wall

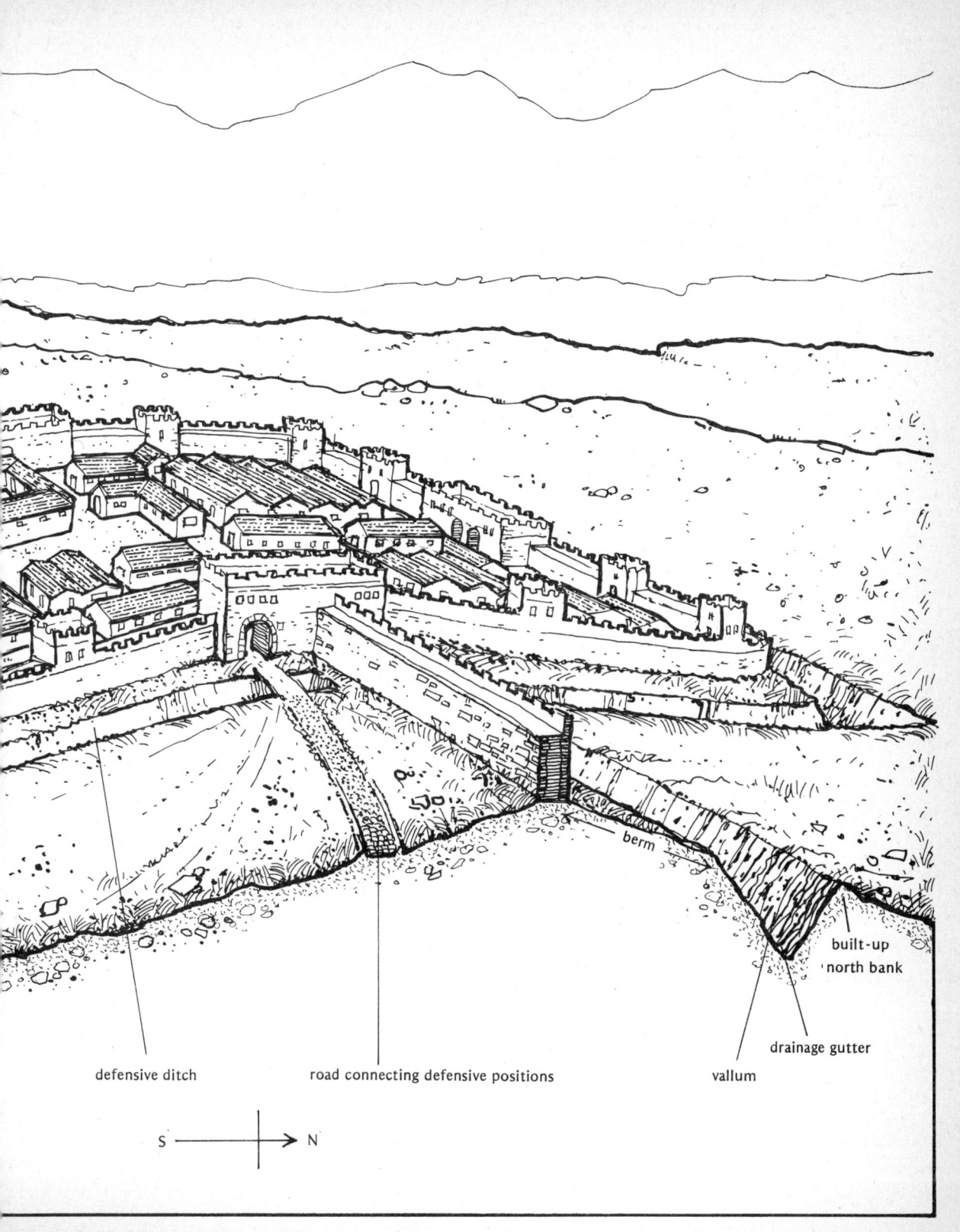

defensive ditch

road connecting defensive positions

vallum

berm

built-up
north bank

drainage gutter

S — N

ROMAN TIMES **Amusements**

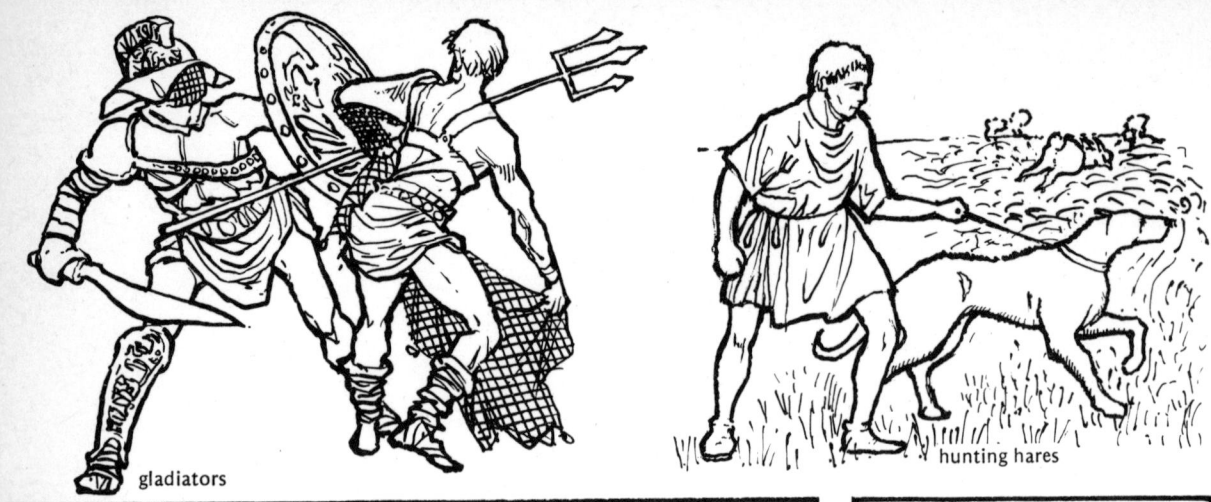

gladiators

hunting hares

TOYS

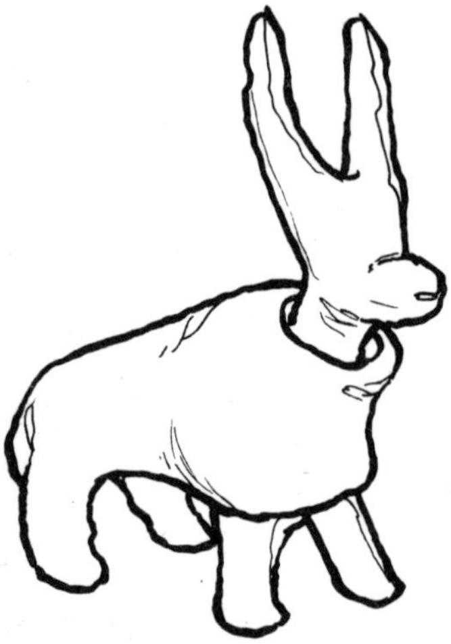

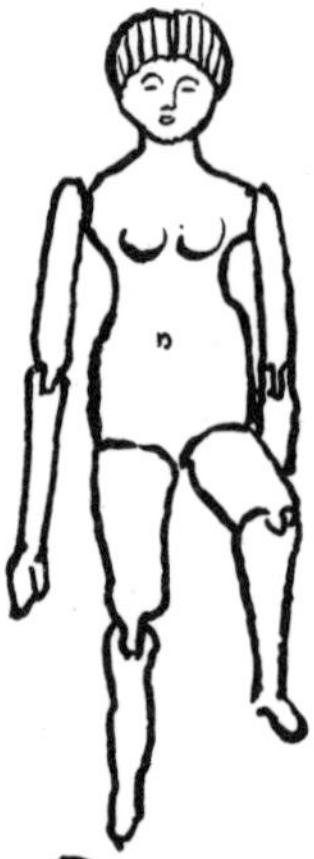

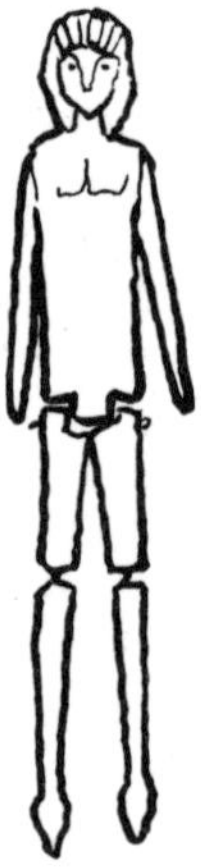

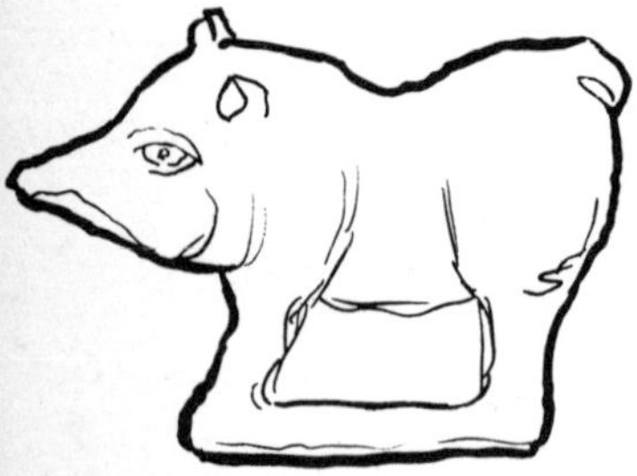

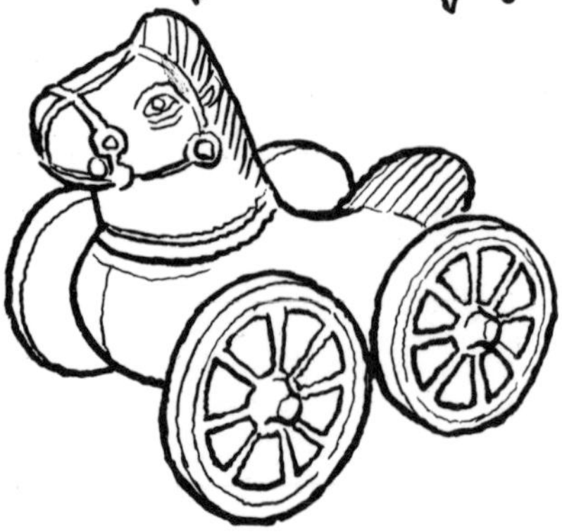

GAMES

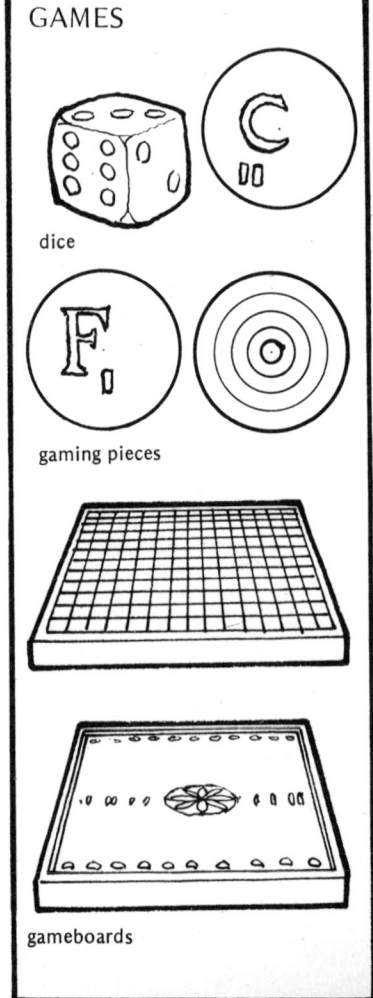

dice

gaming pieces

gameboards

chariot racing

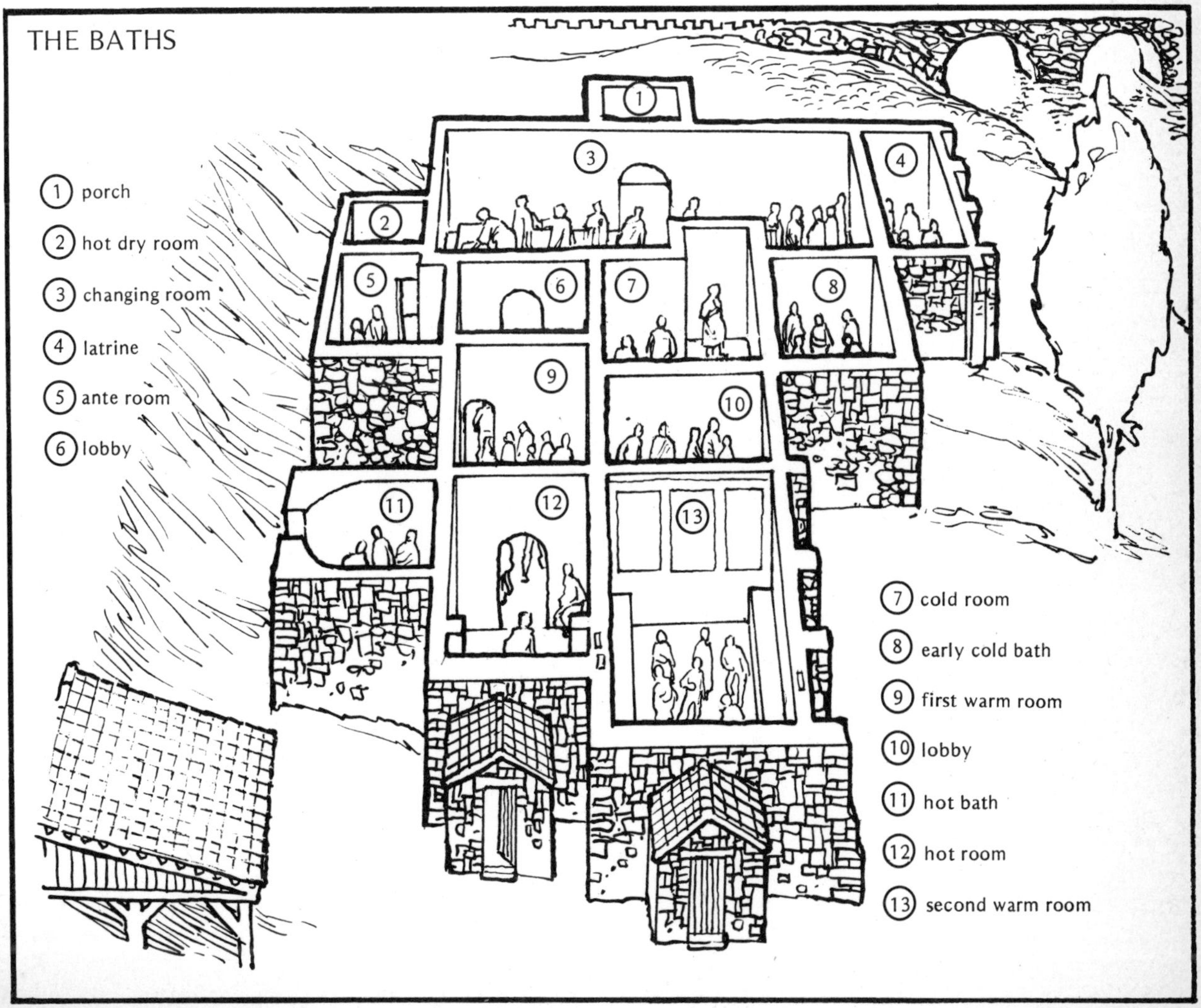

THE BATHS

1. porch
2. hot dry room
3. changing room
4. latrine
5. ante room
6. lobby

7. cold room
8. early cold bath
9. first warm room
10. lobby
11. hot bath
12. hot room
13. second warm room

WRITING

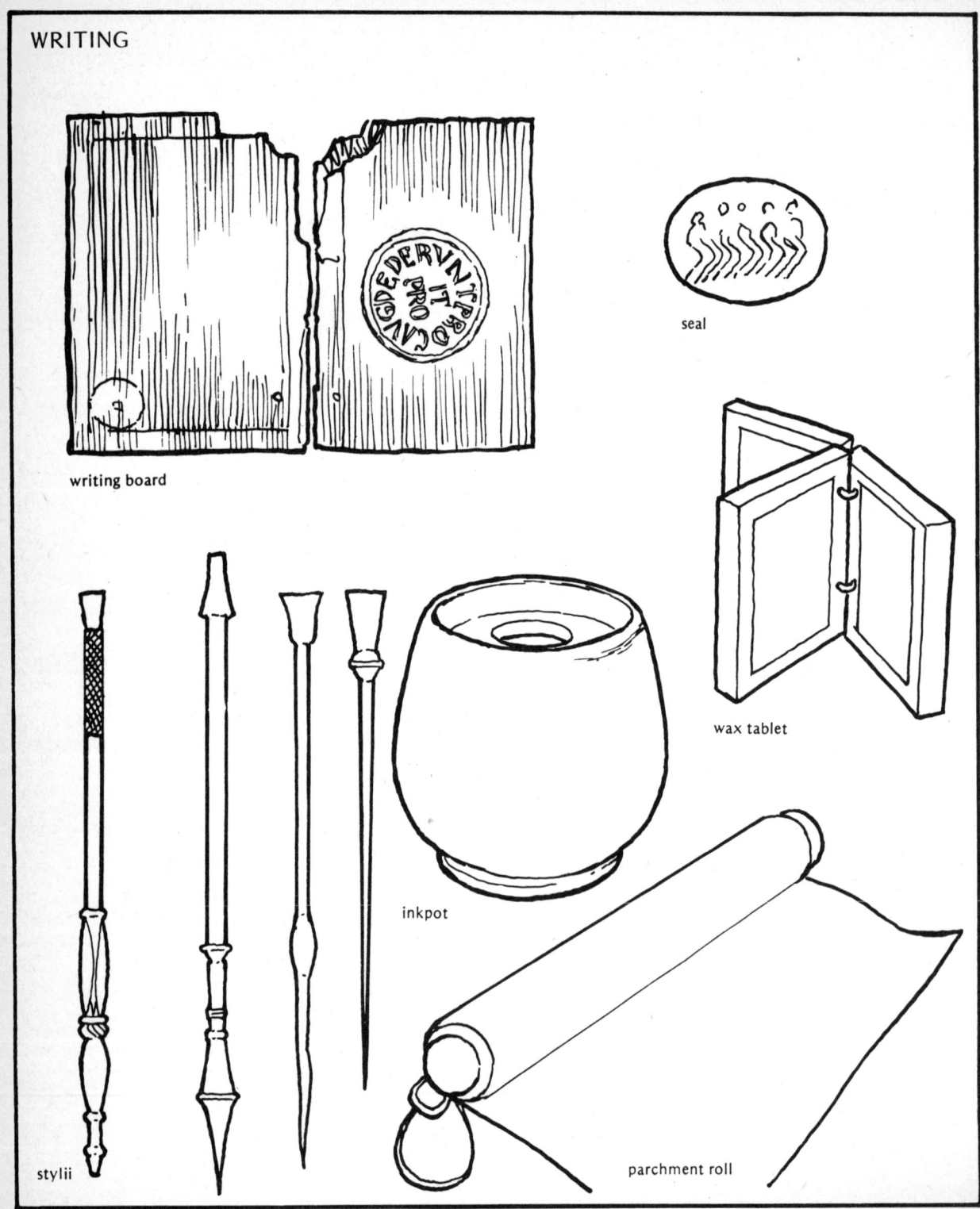

writing board

seal

wax tablet

stylii

inkpot

parchment roll

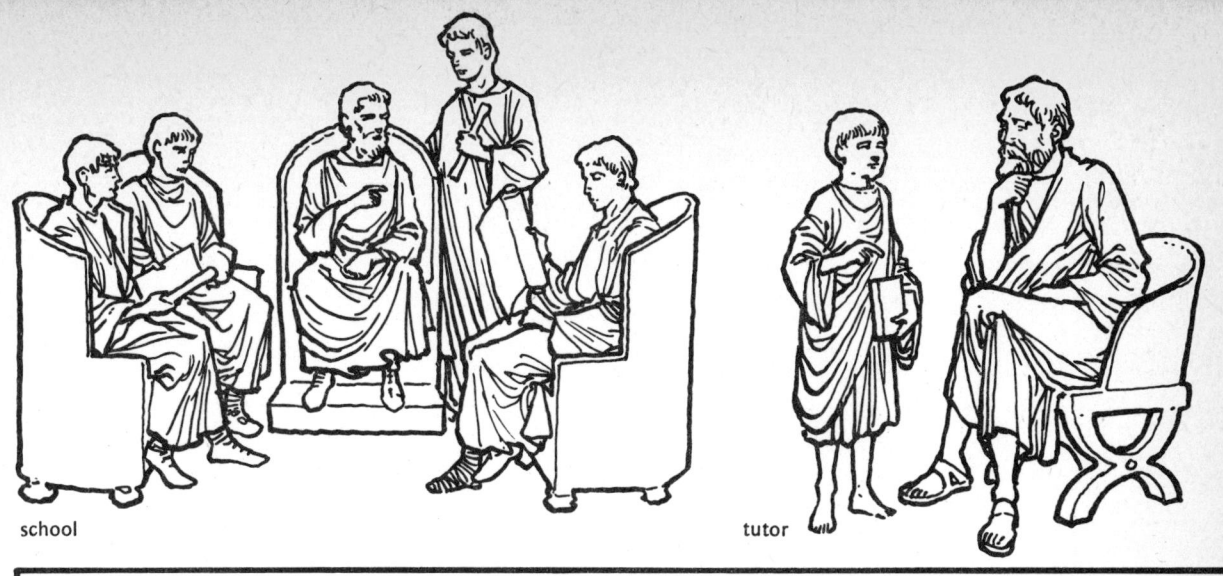

school

tutor

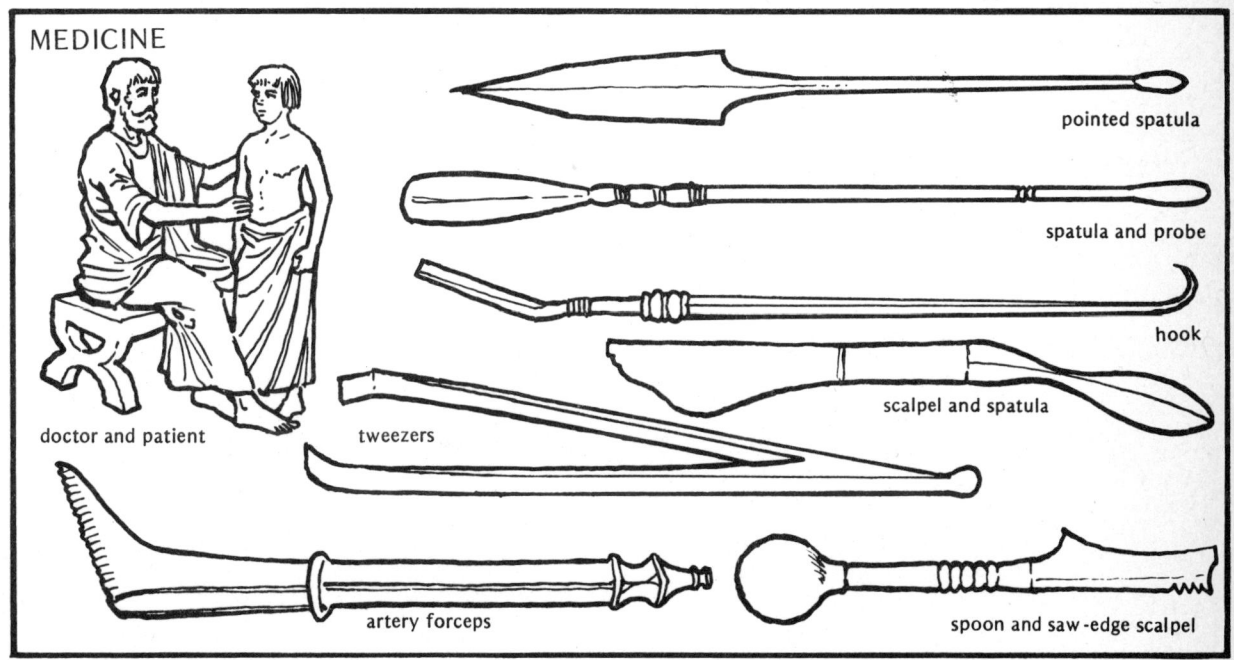

MEDICINE

doctor and patient

tweezers

artery forceps

pointed spatula

spatula and probe

hook

scalpel and spatula

spoon and saw-edge scalpel

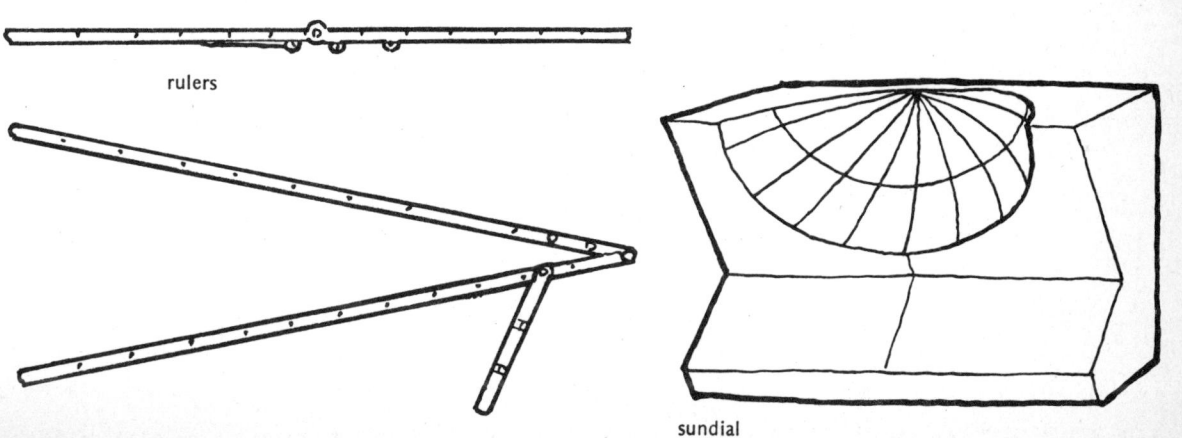

rulers

sundial

ROMAN TIMES   **The Arts**

theatre

STONECARVING

from the Cotswolds

from Hadrian's Wall

from Bath

MUSIC

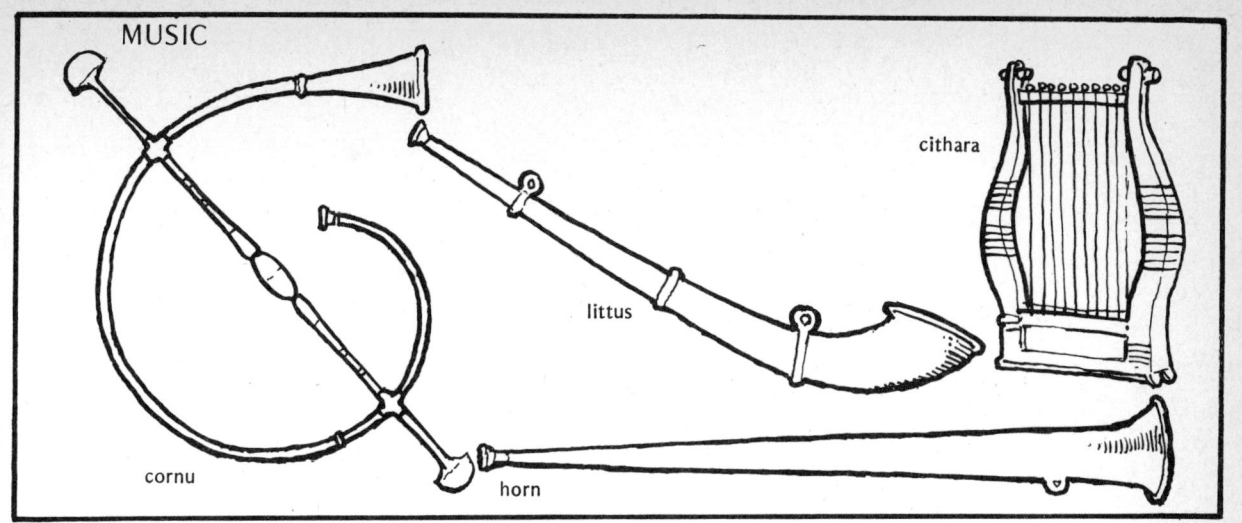

cithara

littus

cornu

horn

MOSAIC DESIGNS

from Fishbourne

from Chedworth

from Brantingham

POTTERY

jug

bowl

SILVER

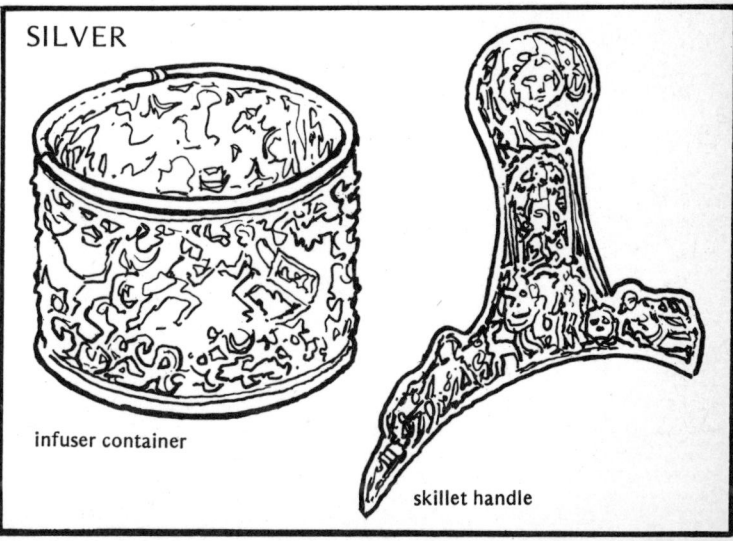

infuser container

skillet handle

ROMAN TIMES   **Some Important Dates**

c 250 BC	First Celtic hill forts
55 BC	Julius Caesar's first expedition to Britain
54 BC	Julius Caesar's second expedition to Britain
AD 43	Claudius starts occupation of Britain
51	Defeat of King Caractacus
60	Boudicca's Revolt; London destroyed
78 – 84	Agricola governor of Britain
122	Hadrian visits Britain
	Building of Hadrian's Wall started
128	Forts on the Wall completed
139	Building of Antonine Wall started
287	Building of Saxon Shore coast defences started
296	Building of Saxon Shore coast defences completed
304	Alban becomes first Christian martyr in Britain
c 410	Last Roman legions leave Britain